I0705269

Fake Gangstas in the Church

by

Larry A. Yff

I was sitting here thinking about the church. I really want to be a part of a church family and do fun church shit...but churches are the perfect example of a dysfunctional family and there's nothing fun about church.

I'm not saying it has to be all fun and games, but damn! Most Christians I see don't look too happy. They don't look like they're having fun sex. They are out there smokin' weed, getting drunk at Happy Hours, addicted to porn, going to strip-clubs, cheating on they taxes and their spouses; basically they're doing the exact same shit they aren't supposed to be doing.

The kicker is they're doing these things while they are telling non-Christians they aren't supposed to be doing them. This may not seem like a big deal because the church has been operating like this for centuries, but I think it's time for a change.

I think it's time for a change only because I finally changed. When I was a Christian and smokin' crack, sniffin' coke, hangin' out at strip-clubs, selling drugs and being involved in gunplay...I was content to be "that Christian". I was a Christian by default: in America you're either a Christian, a Muslim or you're considered to be spiritually lost.

This is serious business because I have officially and publicly aligned myself with all things Bible and am ready to proudly be a frontline Jesus Freak, but I don't feel like I'm marching arm-in-arm with Martin Luther King, Jr and a bunch of other black people and black-friendly white people who challenged police officers who beat them, dogs who wanted to eat them and still took a stand against a country full of millions of mutha fuckas who wanted them all dead and had the legal right to kill them at will.

No. As a Christian, it feels more like I'm walking arm-in-arm with Crazy-Christian Kanye West and the hot black chick who wears the only other "White Lives Matter" shirt that should ever be made, Bugs Bunny and all his friends from Looney Tunes and Homer Simpson.

And to top it off, we're being led by Dora the Explorer who is riding a rainbow-colored unicorn...a unicorn brazenly displaying fake titties with his all-natural, unicorn dick.

Yeah. That's where I'm at and the more I think about it, the more frustrated I get and the more calmer I get. Let me explain...

Christianity is a name that is supposed to be given to anyone who believes in Jesus Christ. Do you see it? Do you see the similarity? Are you connecting the dots? Christianity. Jesus Christ. Christianity. Christ. Christianity. Christians.

You can't just claim to be a Christian and not act like Jesus Christ teaches us we're supposed to be acting.

You can't start a church and not run it the way Jesus Christ said it was supposed to be run.

Claiming to be a Christian is like some of these rappers claiming to be a gangster and they've never put in work. It's like some rapper who grew up in Compton and never did any gang shit, but now that he's famous…he's somehow claiming to be a Blood or a Crip. You can't do that!

I take that back. You *can* do that, but I don't recommend it. Claim to be a gangsta all you want with an album full of a mix of gangster lyrics and love songs if you want to, but one of these days, one of these days, my friend, a true gangster is gonna dog-check yo' ass and make you get back on the porch with the pups where you belong.

I've seen it. I can see it. Everybody except for the mutha fucka claiming to be a gangsta can see it! Quick story…

I was watching this show called "Punk'd". In one episode, they pranked a rapper named Cee Lo. I think his real full name is Cee Lo Green or Charlie Green. Anyways, he is invited to this white family's house as some sort of promotion and doesn't know

it's a prank.

He gets to the house and the little white boy tells Cee Lo

he's a fan and he's stoked about the fact Cee Lo Green is actually

sitting at the dinner table with him. He's excited and tells him,

"Man! Thanks for coming. You're my hero. I look up to you and

it's because of you, I want to rap and have a bunch of bitches like

you!"

The boy's mom looks at him and says, "Tommy! What did

you just say? No. Don't repeat it! Don't repeat it because if you

do, Tommy, I will wash your dirty mouth out with soap, so help

me God!"

The boy looks at his mom and says, "What? What did I say

wrong? Cee Lo is my hero and he has bitches. Don't you Cee Lo?"

as he turns towards Cee. "I love that song where you talk about

pimpin' hoes..."

The boy's mama grabs little Tommy and shakes him.

Tommy starts to fake cry and says to Cee Lo, "I can have bitches

like you, can't I? I can pimp hoes and make money like you, can't

I?"

There's a quiet at the room as all the people at the table

stare at Cee Lo waiting to see what his response will be and here

it comes… "No Tommy. It's not like that," Cee Lo "Charlie" Green

starts off.

"You see, I'm just an entertainer. I've never pimped

anybody. I don't have a lot of women. Cee Lo is my stage name.

My real name is Charlie and I make music and I just rap about

stuff people want to hear. You need to listen to your mom, dude.

I'm just an entertainer…"

Tommy is shocked and starts to run out the room in

disappointment with tears running down his face. As he's getting

ready to leave the room he stops, turns back towards Charlie and says, "Cee Lo. I hate you! I hate you! I wanted to pimp bitches and hoes like you did and you killed my dream! I don't want to be like you anymore!"

I can't tell you what the rest of the video was because I was laughing my ass off! I was crackin' up and had to change the channel because, even though it was funny, it disgusted me and proved a point the majority of adults should know: it takes more than words to be something you claim to be.

I said adults because kids see things differently. They see some guy talking about selling bricks and flippin' pies while he's wearing diamonds and gold and driving a Ferrari...without realizing this mutha fucka never saw a solid kilo of cocaine and used to work at McDonald's flippin' burgers before he got his big break.

The rap game is similar to the church. They are distant cousins. Just take away all the violence, bitches, drug-dealing, killing, gold teeth, diamonds and fast cars and they'd be more like

brothers and sisters.

How can I tie these 2 together? Easy. You have people

like Charlie claiming to be something they're not. They're

claiming to be a certain way and they are leading people down a

bad path.

They are famous and are influencers and have people

think they are real gangsters and people want to be like them not

knowing they're a fake. Just like little, white-boy Tommy in the

example I just showed you, there are millions of people claiming

to be Christian who don't do anything more than attend church

services whenever Football Sundays, the World Series or March

Madness ain't playing on the telly.

That's bad for Christianity. It has people believing they can

just show up for church whenever they want and still do whatever they want...as long as they do their best to hear God's Word being preached whenever their schedule allows it.

Oh yeah, on the flipside, a rapper named The Game was being punked and the guy who hosted the show had to run out from his hiding spot and tell Game it was just a joke and that he was on a prank-show before Game tore some more shit up.

The host was like, "Let's go! Let's go! Everybody stop what you're fucking doing and get out there! We have to let this dude know this is a prank. A joke! Get your asses out there!"

I don't remember his whole prank, but he was pissed. He was pissed and started breakin' shit and telling the fake construction crew that somebody better start giving him some answers or he was gonna fuck all of 'em up.

While we're here, let me give you one more. A famous rapper named T.I. talks a lot about gangsta shit and he got Punk'd on that show.

He apparently was "set up" and made it look like he had a gun or some bullets in one of his bags as he was about to board a plane. The authorities were called and they were telling him he was about to go down for it.

As the "authorities" left to discuss their "findings", the camera zoomed in on T.I. He was fucking terrified. He was like, "I don't know what's going on, but somebody better claim these bullets! I am not about to get in trouble and the minute they come back, I'm going to explain everything to them."

The fake authorities come back and T.I. instantly pulls one of them aside and starts begging and pleading with him and calling him "Sir" and "Dear Sir". I think he even went so far as to start suggesting they question everybody else there and that they should "arrest a certain somebody else" from his staff.

Once again, that shit was hilarious! Now he may well be the gangsta he said he was, but in the face of the Feds...that nigga was shakin' hard! He was shakin' hard and ready to start snitchin'! Funny as shit! Moving on…

Alright, enough of "Punk'd". I done fucked around with so many examples from that silly-ass show I forgot why I was going down that path in the 1st place, but I know it has to have had something to do with God.

I remember! I was letting you know Christians have gotten comfortable; especially in America. With all the "God" stuff on our money, in our courts and the National Anthem, America claims to be a Christian country.

Yeah, right mutha fucka. This is a Christian country where we have allowed so much anti-God and anti-Bible legislation on the books it's a fucking shame! I love America just as much as any American can, but claiming to be a morally conscious nation means you actually have to apply morality in all areas of societal functions.

If you say you are Bible-based in any way, you have to prove it. People have to be able to see you and say, "There's something about him. He's not just a good guy. He's a good guy and for him, his goodness comes from his belief in God."

That's how Christianity is. Wait. No. That's not how it is…that's how it's supposed to be. That's the way it's supposed to operate.

You're not supposed to run around and claim to be a Christian while you don't understand the rules of engagement.

You're not supposed to run around and claim to be a Christian while you're cheating on your husband or wife.

You're not supposed to be a priest in the church and perform sacred rituals while you're performing oral sex on little boys.

What's gonna happen is a real mutha fucka who really loves Jesus is gonna approach you one day. He won't approach you and put a Glock 23 to your head. He will approach you and

ask you to show proof of your set. Proof that you've been living

how Jesus said you're supposed to be livin'.

Are you ready for that? I'm askin' because I wasn't sure I

was ready for that. I was under the impression a Christian simply

meant 1) I went to church, 2) I acknowledged God and Jesus

existed and 3) I am familiar with the Bible.

Ummm, all that means is you went to school in America.

In the United States of America, you can claim to be a Christian

simply from getting a general education. You can claim that

because the national anthem of America says, "God bless

America" and you had to sing it every morning.

American money has, "In God we Trust" printed on it and

when you go to court to testify you have to put your left hand on

a Bible and "promise to tell the truth, the whole truth and nothing

but the truth, so help you God."

BAM! Technically, singing the national anthem means you're a Christian.

BAM! Technically, testifying in court makes you a Christian.

BAM! Technically, you putting faith in the American dollar makes you a Christian.

Do you see how simple entrance into Christianity is? There's no formal blood-in-blood-out type of ritual. There's no testing of your faith in God. There's really no kind of testing of anything other than you saying, "I'm a Christian."

If you can say those 3 words, "I'm a Christian", then you're in! You're officially a Christian! You're qualified to call yourself a Christian and if that's all you've done, I am going to have to politely tell you to get the fuck out the church and leave your badge and church title at the door...please.

There's no way there can be a billion, living Christians on the planet right now and it's operating the way it is. You can't convince me for a second there are a billion people who are all following the laws and lessons found in the Bible and the Lost Books of the Bible and the world is functioning the way it is.

Fuck the world. The United States of America isn't functioning how it's supposed to and I believe there are at least one billion, self-proclaimed Christians here.

I'm gonna take it a step further and say fuck talking about an entire country...it would be hard for me to point to one city in America and say, "Now that's what the fuck I'm talkin' bout! They got some Jesus Freaks running that place! There's more love in the air than pollution and everybody ain't rich...but ain't nobody financially hurtin' either.

It takes a certain strength to stand up for a cause. It seems the harder or more exclusive the entry process is, the more loyalty, pride and productivity occurs.

Look at gang life. Jamaican gangs, Italian gangs, American gangs…they all have a do-or-die process of entering. You don't get to claim something without putting in the work like I said.

Some gangs you have to be able to kill somebody for the gang to get in. Some gangs you have to be able to show your ability to make money. Whatever it is, there is 1st some type of loyalty or earned aspect to entry.

Political parties are no different. If you want to be considered a good Republican or Democrat or whatever your party is, you can get elected, but at some point you have to produce.

At some point you have to be able to show your party you have the ability to throw common sense and morality out the window for the higher cause of the party.

At some point you have to be able to show your party they can count on your vote in the heat of the battle or that you can help them raise money.

This is how life works in every example I could give you with one exception. Christianity.

Christianity seems to be the only organization who actively pursues un-organization.

Christianity seems to be the only organization that thrives on dividing itself up into as many pieces as possible; while thinking they are all one church body in Christ somehow.

Christianity seems to be the only organization that allows membership without any skin in the game and Christianity, in my view, is the only organization that has the power to influence the world and make it a better place.

I became a Christian when I was a couple of months old and my parents had me baptized. I knew nothing of God or religion at the time, but I was given my membership card regardless.

I guess I officially became a Christian when I was around 16 and I had to memorize something from a church document and stand in front of either the church or my church class and formally state my "pledge of allegiance to God and the church".

I can't think of what it was called, but I do know that's all it took. It took some words and since there was no skin in the game, I figured words is all it took to be a Christian.

I was not alone. There were millions of Christians who regularly got fucked up on the weekends.

There were millions of Christians who had drug and porn addictions that remained hidden as best as possible.

There were millions of Christians involved in corporate America who routinely sell products that destroy our human bodies which are supposed to be, according to church protocol, sacred space for the Holy Spirit to dwell in.

There were millions and billions of Christians like that when I was involved in all that activity and there are still millions and billions of Christians like that today.

Am I now pointing my finger and saying they are horrible Christians and they don't deserve to wear the title of Christian. Yes. Yes I am. I'm confidently pointing my index finger at all of them because in doing so…I've got 3 times as many fingers pointing back at myself.

That's how Christianity is supposed to work. It's supposed to be a system where I can say, "Hey, that's not how a Christian is supposed to act" and someone else is supposed to be able to point me out and say, "Hey, that's not how a Christian is supposed to act" and we're all supposed to be able to check each other to keep this Christian thing as pure and powerful as possible.

How do I know this? Because it's in the Constitution of Christianity AKA the Bible. I never looked at it that way until I heard a message by Myles Munroe where he was saying Christianity was a political organization by design and not a religious one.

He went on to say every political body has a code of operation and not only that, the code is written for everyone to follow. Everyone member of that body is expected to live according to those laws and be protected under those laws.

According to those laws, Christians are supposed to, "...confess your sins to each other and pray for each other so that you may be healed. The prayer of a righteous person is powerful

and effective…"

Christians aren't following basic laws and that is what is

basically keeping the church body in its' present, weakened state.

How many of you know of a Christian who is out there publicly

confessing his or her sins BEFORE they get caught and asking for

help from within the church community?

I'll bet none. Nobody wants to admit to being a Christian

and watching porn.

Nobody wants to admit to being a Christian and being

involved in homosexual activity.

Nobody wants to admit to being a Christian and having an

alcohol problem.

There is so much hidden shit in the church it's ridiculous.

Once again, the Christian lifestyle is designed to be universally

beneficial. The Bible is telling us we are legally supposed to take action when we have a problem or addiction by sharing it with someone else.

We're supposed to share not for the sake of sharing, but for the sake of being delivered! Whenever a Christian has a problem, he or she can legally be delivered by simply admitting it to someone else in the church and praying with each other for healing! Damn! That's simple! It's legal and simple and Christians aren't doing it.

Christians aren't doing it, but non-Christians aren't either. This book isn't about non-Christians, so I don't want to get too side-tracked. Since I already mentioned it, I will say if you are not a Christian, how does the prospect of being delivered from an addiction by simply confessing it and praying over it sound to you?

If it sounds good, give it a try. That's all saying. I'm all about God and the Bible, but I'm not all about saying it's the only way.

You have to find your way and one of the best ways to find a good way is to look for good examples of people living their best life in a certain way. You get what I'm sayin'?

You should be able to see in the news, in the church and in movies real-life examples of this type of power working. I'm not mad at you if you think Christianity is full of shit and irrelevant because personally, we are on the same page.

I am constantly looking for public examples somewhere, anywhere, where I can tell someone, "Look at him. That's what you can legally expect to have happen when you do it according to the Bible." I can't find any and part of that is on me.

I can't tell someone to look for examples of the true power of the Bible when I'm not being an example. I should be able to keep my mouth shut and have people look at my life and say, "I'm

interested in how he fully recovered from addictions to porn and

cocaine. He said he did it and his life shows it. He says God did it

and if God can do all the stuff I see going on in his life, maybe this

Christian-stuff is worth looking in to."

Kirk Franklin. He is a gospel singer I've mentioned a couple

of times because of his addiction to porn. He openly confessed

about his massive porn collection, but it wasn't in the most

voluntary way Christians are supposed to do it.

The thing about a Christian is you're supposed to openly

confess and share. It's technically not "openly confessing and

sharing" when you get caught.

Kirk got caught and THEN he opened up about his porn

addiction. There's a big difference, but I guess in the end he

technically followed the Bible's instruction.

I also saw a pastor recently who was getting lots of views for admitting he was cheating on his wife. Once again, he is being given a lot of credit for opening up and sharing about it, but he is only doing it AFTER he got caught cheating again.

Listen, getting caught is not openly confessing. Talking about something after you get caught is simply admitting to guilt. He was sincere, but I'm just saying it's a much better example when you confess something without being caught.

There was one last incident I wanna share with you. There was a pastor in Montana or somewhere in that part of America I think, who was on stage "openly confessing to a sexual sin and openly humbling himself and asking his congregation to forgive him."

Sounds good, huh? It sounds like that's the right thing for a pastor in the church to do and he's being a good example, right?

Wrong. I say wrong because he wasn't confessing shit...he was admitting guilt.

Apparently he had been sleeping with some female in the church in his church office since she was a young teen, borderline tween. He got busted and THEN he decided to openly confess.

He was on stage talking about it and being all humble until the girl stood up and said in front of everybody that she was the young teen girl he was talking about and that she hated his fucking guts and that he defiled her in a way she never imagined.

He was teaching her how to do all kinds of sexual shit and some of it was shit she never knew about. She also told everybody how she hates how he took advantage of his position to manipulate her.

This was going on for years and she was tired of it. She was tired of it and she was tellin' it all and tellin' it in front of everybody! People all over the place had they cellphones out!

Her husband stood by her side and they both walked up to the stage hand-in-hand. I thought this young buck was gonna beat the pastor's ass. Instead, he gave the pastor a piece of his mind as well.

If there was ever a time somebody was gonna get publicly beaten up, that was it. I didn't think he was gonna survive it, but he did and here's the thing…he didn't get offered forgiveness from the girl, her husband or any of the people in the church until he actually confessed.

They weren't playing that partial shit! He stood there with his head down a little bit and was staring at his shoes. The girl was in his face and she wanted some healing and she wanted it now!

The Bible says to openly confess and get healed. He wasn't giving her what he wanted by saying, "Yeah, I want to admit I had sex with a young member of my church and I'm asking

for forgiveness" and that, Reader, is not a complete confession.

The kind of confession that heals is full confession. She

said, more liked screamed in his face, "I don't care about you

saying you had sex with a young girl. I'm that young girl! Say my

name! I want you to say to everyone here, 'I had sex with Mary

Ann from the time she was 14 until she was 18.' That's what I

need to hear!'

Everybody in the church was like, "Yeah! You owe her that

much!" others were like, "Say it! Say her name!" and her husband

was like, "Give my wife what she deserves so she can heal. You

owe her that much!"

The pastor still found it extremely hard to say because

certain confessions, especially dealing with sex or porn or young

people or Heaven forbid, all 3! Those types of confessions seem to require a sort of humbling and faith in God that is on another level.

That type of shit is typically gonna remain hidden for life. It tends to come out when you get a bunch of money because you can pay for privacy. You can pay to live out any fetish you want with money and people will help you live them out because they are somehow benefitting from it financially.

I didn't wind up watching the whole video, but when I stopped watching, he was still at the point of actively only being able to admit to the act. Putting a name on it makes it personal and very hard to admit.

As a Christian and one who is pointing out his example, I can understand exactly what he's talking about. I can feel his pain and I can fully understand why he was finding the floor and his shoes so interesting during his interrogation.

In case you don't know, I had a porn addiction. I allowed it to go so deep, dark and crazy that I was starting to look at young girls. Confessing that was kind of easy to do, but having to confess it with an actual person...that shit is borderline impossible!

Ouch!!! Triple ouch!!! You know what, Reader, we'll take time away from whatever track we were on for me to give you an open confession of a very hard nature. I'm only able to give it to you because I already cracked it open in real life...

I had a friend of mine who was in the church and she had a young daughter I had met in real life. She was around 12 or 13. I never made any sexual passes at her or touched her or no shit like that BUT, at some point of me watching porn, I would think about her sexually.

Now, nothing ever happened, but I did talk with her mother before and explained that situation to her. She was familiar with some type of porn or sexual abuse in her family and was somewhat understanding and somewhat forgiving…as forgiving as a mom could be, I suppose.

I could only imagine if I had gotten to the point of actually approaching her and having sex with her! Damn! If that had happened, my open confession would have gotten a whole lot harder and if I'm honest with myself, it would probably never have been an open confession unless I got caught somehow or she got pregnant.

I'm staying on this topic for a while because of the destructive nature of porn and sex in society. In reality, the billions of Christians who are involved in sexual irresponsibility and addictions are supposed to be able to legally correct it with a simple confession, prayer and faith in God who the prayer is being sent to.

I was a Christian when I was involved in killing a baby via abortion...and I wasn't the only one.

I was having sex with married women while I was a Christian...and I wasn't the only one.

I was going to strip-clubs while I was a Christian...and I wasn't the only one.

Basically, as a Christian, I was involved in killing babies as a result of being involved in sex that goes against my Constitution. I was destroying and disrespecting a God-ordained and respected institution called marriage by being involved in sex that goes against my Constitution. I was viewing woman as pieces of meat and something just to lust after and have sex with because I was going against my Constitution.

I'm here to tell you if all the millions and billions of people who claimed to be Christians would start living according to the Constitution they are confessing to be legally bound by, that would eliminate millions of babies being killed and millions of homes, families and marriages being ruined and billions of dollars from being spent on sex-trafficking and porn.

And that's only the sexual duties and responsibilities of Christians. I haven't even touched on other areas like business, how to help financially poor people and other topics.

One simple change from trying to create and follow our own laws to actually following God's laws would result in a massive, positive change in society.

Let's get away from the sex stuff and talk about the power Christians are always blabbing and running their mouths about and have no ideal what it requires. Ready?

Have you ever heard a Christian quote Psalm 23? If you're unfamiliar with it, it goes something like this: **The Lord is my shepherd. I shall not want. He makes me lie down in green pastures and leads me beside quiet waters, He refreshes my**

soul. He guides me along the right paths for His name's sake.

Even though I walk through the valley of the shadow of death, I

will fear no evil, for you are with me; your rod and your staff

they comfort me. You prepare a table before me in the presence

of my enemies. You anoint my head with oil; my cup overflows.

Surely your goodness and love will follow me all the days of my

life and I will dwell in the house of the Lord forever.

And that's one of the most common things from the Bible Christians love to quote but don't actually believe. Do you know why I say they don't believe? It's pretty simple when you take a basic, simple-ass look at passages in the Bible and take them to heart. Watch this...

- **The Lord is my shepherd. I shall not want.** How many Christians do you know who believe they have everything they want? How many of you who are Christians believe your faith in God has put you in the current position to have everything you want? Christians are supposed to be some of the most content, satisfied people in the world…if they really believe in this passage, right?

- **He guides me along the right paths for His namesake.** How many Christians are out there giving God glory for their success? And when I pose that question, I'm not talking about someone who gets an award and says, "I first want to thank God and give Him all the glory…" I'm talking about someone who is living a life full of success and they're constantly talking about God guiding them down a certain path in life instead of talking about how they are self-made or that they did all the right things or that they worked hard and didn't give up. How many of those people are Christians who tell everyone they "were guided by guide" down the career path they chose? How many Christians can you name who have a business that is designed to be profitable and publicly give God glory?

- **I will fear no evil. You prepare a table for me in the presence of my enemies.** How many Christians are fearless? How many Christians are bold in the face of persecution? How many Christians are unmoved and unafraid of the "war on terrorism"? Christians love to quote this as a favorite scripture, but how many would feel comfortable eating with their enemies? Do you know how comfortable you gotta be to be able to sit down and enjoy a nice peaceful meal in the presence of your enemies and haters?

What I wanted to show you with the famous Psalm 23 is how you should be feeling and acting if you know God is on your side. That Psalm shows absolute confidence. A confidence in the face of death. A confidence in the presence of enemies. This Psalm emanates confidence...a confidence very few Christians have.

There is a scripture about God making your cup overflow and Christians love to talk about it and get excited. Yes! Yes, God promised to give me more wealth and riches than I can handle! Yeah God!

What they failed to realize, and what a lot of preachers failed to teach, is God did promise that BUT you 1st had to bring your full tithe to the church.

That means if your gross paycheck was $2,000 and after taxes you took home $1,300, your tithe is still $200. That's your full tithe.

Your full tithe is to be done based on the same dollar amount the government takes their cut. You don't let the government take out 34% of your check and then out of that you give God 10%.

If you want the wealth and riches God was talking about, you have to give the government their 34% and God His 10% and then you live off the rest. In that example I just gave, how many

Christians do you think actually give the full tithe?

I know I didn't. I used to feel good being able to just put

something in the plate that was green. I would get take home

about $300 a week and when it would come time for tithe, I

would "go big" and put a $10-dollar bill in the plate. That would

make me feel good knowing I didn't just throw a couple of singles

in there.

You see, if you follow the Constitution like you're

supposed to, then yes, God is required to do exactly what He says

in it. That's the beauty of the Bible!

It is a Constitution that is backed by God. It not only lays

out His laws for citizens of Heaven, it also provides historically

accurate examples of what people received who followed the law

or didn't follow the law. It lays out all kinds of examples to help

you make the best decision possible.

How many government Constitutions do that? How many Constitutions stay the same and interpreted the same regardless of what political party is in office?

In America, the Constitution is enforced differently by the United States Supreme Court Justices based on what their political party association is. That's why there's so much controversy and fighting over appointed Justices to that court.

It is the highest court in America and once a judge is appointed, he or she is appointed for life. There is so much fighting, bribing and mud-slinging around an appointment because of control

In the human system of politics, humans are constantly jockeying for positions of power. Everybody wants to try and control legislation so they can make as much money for them, their party and people who financial support them.

In the spiritual system of politics, God is in charge and has all the power and His laws are laid out to reward and punish people equally regardless of skin color, economic position, political party or any other factors. That's my kind of government!

There is an act called sacrifice. A sacrifice is part physical and part spiritual. It can be simple or elaborate based on the situation and desired outcome.

Humans have been sacrificing to spiritual beings since Adam was created. In fact, since God said the cost of sinning is death, once Adam sinned, he threw all humanity under a system of sacrifice.

Sin requires sacrifice. Instead of Adam or any other human dying, God allowed them, in His system, to sacrifice an animal that was blemish-free as a way of representing a pure blood sacrifice.

Once Jesus shed His blood, He became the human who released all humanity from the system of sacrificing and gave control of the world back to human. They had legally lost it to sin.

Humanity had not given control of the world's systems over to Satan...they gave it over to sin. Satan loves to encourage and influence us to sin because he hates God and us and he wants us to choose sin.

Now that Jesus gave us control over sin, did you know if you believe in that sacrificing process I just told you about, you legally are able to get back everything you lost? Yes. You LEGALLY can get everything back you lost as a result of the reversal of Adam's actions.

You see, this is where it gets complicated, spiritual and deep. Your average Christian doesn't want to go this deep into studying God and the legal aspect of Jesus' life and death and that's also why the average Christian isn't enjoying life and peace

the way Jesus came to show them how to live.

Christians love to sing songs and hear sermons about Jesus

healing people...and then don't believe Jesus can heal them.

Don't believe me? Check this out...

I wasn't feeling good recently and decided to try

something new. I turned to the Bible and saw where it said, "If

any of you are sick, call an elder in the church and he will pray

over you and anoint you with holy oil and you will be healed."

I reached out to an elder at my church and said I wanted

to see him to get healed like the Bible said. I didn't have his

phone number, so I sent him a message through Facebook

Messenger.

He messaged me back and said he wouldn't be available

for a couple of days and since he still wanted me to get some healing, he said he would do the next best thing…he sent me a prayer text.

A prayer text? I'm supposed to get healed from a sickness with a text message?

Pastors preach and teach lovely stories about Jesus healing that one woman who had a lifetime blood disease and the crowd erupts in cheers and excitement every time and start shouting, "Yes God. Yes Jesus. I know you can do it. Heal me too Lord!"

And then they run out and get every vaccination and booster and re-booster shot big drug companies have to offer. I mean, that's a fake gangsta.

You're running around talking about how you believe Jesus can heal you, but instead of going through Christian protocol to get healed, you wear double-masks for protection and inject yourself with all kinds of vaccines and don't talk to people and don't go to church and stay in the house.

Is that how you're supposed to live if you believe in the healing power Jesus has? Did He do all that healing and get all them stripes on His back so you can walk around scared and depressed?

Christians have access to a healing power others don't. It's a simple process of having faith in Jesus. You know him, right? You are a Christian, right?

He's the person behind the name Christianity. He is the one who healed people with deadly diseases like leprosy and said He can show you how to do the same.

He's the person behind the name Christianity that told Christians He can heal any sickness, but somehow, Christians believe in Jesus but don't believe He can handle COVID. They believe He may be good, but not that good.

That's being a fake gangsta. How are you going to say you believe Jesus can heal you from diseases and sickness and you would rather trust science and vaccines over the blood of Jesus?

I get it though. I used to just want to be a Christian, go to church when I got the chance and made sure I didn't get involved in anything that looked like it went against God. But that's where most Christians, including myself fuck up…

Your level of "not going against God" is based on your level of knowing God. If you know God personally, you would know you don't want alcohol in your system. Why? Because the Holy Spirit who Jesus had God send to guide us, somehow has access to our bodies as a spiritual guide.

If our body isn't functioning properly due to alcohol and we're doing things under the influence that definitely register as sin, then we are going against God. But you see what just happened, Reader? I'll tell you…

What happened was being a Christian got too deep again.

Nobody wants to be reminded about sinning. That shit ain't no

fun!

What people want is to be able to say they love God

without ever getting to know Him, Jesus or the Holy Spirit. I did

this in a different book, but this is a good place to insert a short,

Private Matter Bonus Essay about getting personal with God,

Jesus and the Holy Spirit. Check it out and then we'll get right

back on track:

Christian Trinity...Christian Tragedy

The Church tells Believers that a personal relationship

with God and Jesus is the ultimate goal. That's fine and all, but

you can't say that and then not explain to us who God is because

you think it's a tricky subject.

I've asked several people from pastors to old-timer

Believers to please describe who God is. The best answer I've

gotten is that He is a personality and so is Jesus and so is the

Holy Spirit.

So, let me get this straight: my goal is to get personal

with a personality that is somehow made up of 3 personalities?

Not gonna happen. Impossible.

I don't know why the religious leaders avoid this subject

so much. The more they ignore this important topic, the more I

see why Jesus despised the religious leaders of His day. He was

always getting into it with them and calling them snakes.

How about this: God is our Father and He is a Being. We

are made in His image and He walks and talks and has arms and

legs like us. He is NOT Jesus and when Jesus came to Earth, He

was NOT God in an earthly body.

The Holy Spirit, God and Jesus are 3 separate Beings. Once I looked at like that, I was finally able to get personal with all 3 in our own way. And I have to admit it felt *extremely* good and my walk with them finally became a reality! I was able to tap into the Father-Son relationship with God by following the example Jesus gave us.

He was always talking about doing what His dad told Him to because He loves His dad and His dad loves Him. Viewing God as a 3-Being, shape-shifter will never get you to the point where you can get personal with Him because you can't get personal with a cloud.

The image of the holy trinity has helped Satan because it keeps us from getting a personal relationship with God. Jesus told us to pray to our Father who is in Heaven. That clearly means Him and God aren't the same Being. He also said, you can talk about me but anybody that talks about the Holy Spirit has committed the only sin that is unforgivable.

Moses was bold and asked God if he could see Him. God

said that would be impossible because His glory is too bright.

But He did tell Moses He would WALK past him and cover Moses

up WITH HIS HANDS so he wouldn't try and look at God's face.

God then said, I will uncover you so you can see my BACK as I

WALK on to wherever He was headed.

There it is. God has a body, arms, back, legs and a face.

Please get personal with Him on a one-on-one basis and stop

believing the trinity teaching that God is a 3-Being personality or

a mysterious, impersonal "thing" that is made up of 3 other

"things."

Who's your daddy? God is!

And that's all I'll say about my thoughts about the Trinity.

Once again, I wasn't always thinking along these lines. I wasn't

because it takes too much time and I was a busy man.

If you want to get to know God it takes time. You now not only have to try and understand how physical things work in your life. You now also have to understand how the spiritual aspect of your life works.

Not only that, but now you have to understand who these unseen, spiritual beings are and what spiritual warfare really means.

Not only that, but once you get a basic handle of spiritual beings and warfare, you now have to find out how to operate in the physical and spiritual realm simultaneously.

Not only that, you have to be on guard every day for spiritual attacks as well as physical attacks such as being robbed, assaulted or having somebody plotting to undermine you in a business deal or take your job at work.

Do you see why spiritual understanding isn't something Christians aren't quick to take up? It was so much easier for me when I could just say I was a Christian.

It was easier for me to show how much I loved God by making sure I went to church whenever I could. Some people aren't satisfied with showing others and God how good of a Christian they are by simply going to church; they also have to become deacons, elders and be included on the Prayer Team.

Somehow, Christians have been fooled into believing the more time they spend working for the church, the better and stronger their faith is and that's not what builds faith.

I've asked pastors, deacons and elders who God is and I've gotten answers from, "Well, nobody really knows" to "That's a subject we don't like to talk about at church because it's too complicated".

Complicated? Understanding God on a personal level is essential in the respect process and you're telling me it's too complicated? How about this, Reader. Do me a favor and ask as many Christians you know to describe God and see what you come up with.

I'll tell you:

- God is everywhere at once

- Jesus is God in the flesh

- God, Jesus and the Holy Spirit are the 3 personalities that make up the entity we call God

The bottom line is you have to put in the work, time and effort to support a commitment in life. You have to decide if you wanna be a fake gangsta or a real one.

Do you want to be a Christian and put in the work or just tell people you're a Christian?

That is a very important question you need to answer for yourself. As someone who was a fake gangsta in the church, I'm hear to tell you, being real is much better!

It ain't gonna be easy, but then again, shit you get easy is often the cheapest, most unproductive way to get it. This Jesus walk is serious business. Being a Christian is about being powerful and having influence...not for personal gain, but to give God glory.

That wraps it up for me. I already included a Private Matter Bonus Essay about the Trinity in the body of the book, so now, I'm just gonna include one here. Check it out:

JESUS FREAK

There is a term thrown around called "Jesus Freak". It was designed to be a put-down on anybody who was seriously into

Jesus. It worked. Well, it worked for a little while. I have to admit, it even worked on me…at first.

Following the Bible and being a Christian has always been a social and religious target for people who want to live life on their own terms. Nobody ever attacks Islam, Buddhism, Darwinism but if you mention you are a Christian or if you mention the name "Jesus", here come the sighs and the "why do you always have to talk about Jesus?" reactions.

Here's why. You know what? I was going to do it in paragraph form, but I just changed my mind. I like list's so I'm going to number some of the reasons why:

1.	Jesus is the only human who ever claimed to know God directly and He had plenty of supporting evidence with His actions.

2.   Jesus is the only human ever whose death was documented and witnessed by many people...and His resurrection was also witnessed and documented by many people.

3.   Jesus is the only human that had documented records where He was able to tell storms to die down and to control nature.

4.   Jesus is the only human who delivered a message that talked about getting personal with the creator of the Universe. All other religious and spiritual paths talk about some "thing" that is not designed for humans to get personal with (Islam being an exception...kind of).

5.   Jesus is the only human who is recorded as performing actual miracles. Miracles that included raising people from the dead.

6.   Jesus is the only human who gave us a clear explanation for human's purpose on Earth AND tied it into our spiritual origins. All other spiritual walks just tell us to do what we think is right and love everybody and we're gonna be A-ok.

7.   Jesus is the only human who has recorded and documented manuscripts written thousands of years before His birth that predicted His coming.

I could go on forever with this list, but I won't. I think you get the point that Jesus was and is an extraordinary individual. He spent His adult life here on Earth looking out for us. His laser-focus was to let us know that God is real, Satan and sin are real and that since He is the only one who actually witnessed Earth's beginnings and the rise and fall of Satan and sin, His goal was to teach us how to duplicate the Kingdom of Heaven here on Earth.

He also had a ton of lessons about life that, if followed properly, will make any individual find peace, happiness and success in every situation in life. He tied right, wrong, good, bad, God, Heaven, financial and spiritual wealth together in a way that no one before Him or since Him has been able to do.

If somebody wants to label me as a "Jesus Freak", I gladly accept that title. Actually, you can call me whatever the fuck you want to and I won't be offended or mad. In the case of the "Jesus Freak" label, I will actually shake your hand and thank you. That's a label I will gladly wear.

I have to say something about the "Jesus Freak" thing. A lot of people are finding it fashionable to wear bracelets that say "what would Jesus do" and people like to make social media posts that say "I love Jesus and He is My Lord and Savior. If you agree, please share." And now you got 3,000 mutha fuckas agreeing...but are they actually living like Jesus wants them to?

Do you remember the Lord's prayer? A lot of Believers say that prayer daily or at least a lot. How many of them understand that our purpose on Earth is to create Heaven on Earth? In that prayer, Jesus taught us to ask for "...may your Kingdom come..." That means we are asking for the Kingdom of Heaven to be established on Earth.

How does God work on Earth? Since He gave humans dominion, He rarely just comes in and does whatever He wants to do. He respects His own laws. What God looks for is for humans that He can work through.

The entire Bible if full of recorded events where God has Moses free the slaves, Joshua leading battles and prophets to give messages to world leaders and specific groups of people.

Jesus constantly told people who were interested in His lessons that they had to take action. Believers are supposed to suit up for spiritual warfare. Believers are supposed to stand up against laws that go directly against God's laws such as the legalization of homosexual marriage, corrupt and prejudicial drug sentencing laws and a host of other activity that certain members of society try and legalize so they can try and operate above God's laws.

A real "Jesus Freak" is ready to stand up when the rest of society is bowing down to social pressure. A "Jesus Freak" is an individual who doesn't just wear a *Jesus t-shirt* while he or she is actively involved in activities that destroy our temple such as drinking, vaping and letting their bodies get completely out of shape.

I will close with this: "Jesus Freaks" are the true leaders of society. Don't try and wear this badge without putting in the time. Being a "Jesus Freak" is not designed to be a fad. It involves daily prayer, meditation and conversations with our Heavenly Father, with Jesus and with the Holy Spirit.

The key word is "daily". A true "Jesus Freak" does not go to church one hour a week and think that their "God time" quota for the week is satisfied. You don't get to wear the "Jesus Freak" label if that's the only time you tryin' to put in.

"Jesus Freaks", it's time to run shit!!!

It's time to stop being scared to stand up for shit!!!

It's time to stop letting human governments that

contradict Heaven's government to continue to fuck shit up!!!

It's time to re-claim your lost shit!!! It's time to start a

local Bible Fight Club!!! It's time to do whatever your "Jesus"

shirts are telling the world that you do!!!

LET'S DO THIS SHIT FOR REAL, JESUS FREAKS!!!

I'll see the rest of you freaks at the finish line!!!

Personal Development Notes

Personal Development Notes

www.ingramcontent.com/pod-product-compliance
Lightning Source LLC
Chambersburg PA
CBHW071215260726
48653CB00041B/860